LAUREATE SERIES

MMO 4047

T0156377

Aria: Ombra mai fù
(Serse)

G.F. Handel

Om – – – bra mai_ fú — di ve-ge - ta-bi-le

Cara, Cara e Dolce

Alessandro Scarlatti

Allegretto grazioso — p legato — mf

Ca-ra, ca-ræ dol-ce — Ca-ra, ca-ræ

If Music Be the Food of Love

Henry Purcell

Gently — p — cresc.

If mu - sic be the food of love Sing on, sing on, sing

The Lovely Milleress
(Die Schöne Müllerin)
1. Wandering (Das Wandern)

Franz Schubert

Das Wan –dern ist des Mül-lers Lust, das Wan – dern! Das

Duna

Josephine McGill

When I was a lit-tle lad With fol - ly on my

There Is A Balm in Gilead

Arranged by
George Shirley

There is a balm in Gi - le-ad to

Music Minus One

MMO CD 4047
MMO Cass. 9031

LAUREATE SERIES BEGINNING TENOR SOLOS
BEGINNING LEVEL FOR TENOR SOLOS

Band No. Complete Version		Band No. Minus Voice	Page No.
1	*Handel:* Aria: Ombra mai fù	7	4
2	*Scarlatti:* Cara, Cara e Dolce	8	6
3	*Purcell:* If Music Be The Food Of Love	9	8
4	*Schubert:* The Lovely Merress	10	10
5	*McGill:* Duna	11	13
6	*Spiritual:* There Is A Balm In Gilead	12	17

9031

PERFORMANCE GUIDE

G. F. HANDEL
Ombra mai fù (*Xerxes*)

George Frederic Handel was born in 1685, in the same year as Johann Sebastian Bach. Handel was a prolific composer of opera, oratorio, and instrumental music. "Ombra mai fù" is the first aria of the opera *Serse* (*Xerxes*), which was written in 1738. In the opera, the aria is sung by Xerxes in a beautiful garden in which a plane-tree is growing. He sings, "There never was a lovelier tree than thou, there never was a sweeter shade of a dear and lovely plant."

The first sound of "Ombra" must be floated with a lovely lyric sound, with a slight crescendo or "warming" of the tone. The effect of the aria is dependent on a free and floating vocal sound from beginning to end. Sing the final "Di vegetabile cara ed amabile" broadly, with a full resonant tone and a well sustained fermata on the high F in measure 44.

ALESSANDRO SCARLATTI
Cara, cara e dolce

Alessandro Scarlatti, born in Palermo, Italy in 1660, was an important composer of the Neapolitan school. He is credited with the establishment of the school of *bel canto,* laying the foundation for the modern Italian opera. To Scarlatti, melody was of primary importance. "Cara, cara e dolce" ("Dear, Dear and Sweet") is a fine example of his graceful melodic style. Attention must be given to pure vowels and to a clear articulation of sixteenth notes.

HENRY PURCELL
If Music Be the Food of Love

Henry Purcell, one of England's greatest composers, was born in 1659. It has been said that he was the first professional composer, since he wrote music only on commission. Purcell's prosody was especially masterful. Be aware of the bass line in the accompaniment, as it determines the harmonic basis of the song. Clarity of diction and maintenance of a long and flexible vocal line are of utmost importance.

FRANZ SCHUBERT
Das Wandern

Franz Schubert, born in Vienna in 1797, remains not only the most prolific, but also the greatest, of all song writers. "Das Wandern" ("The Wanderer") is the opening song of Schubert's song cycle, *Die Schöne Müllerin,* set to a text by Wilhelm Müller. The mood of the song is happy and carefree, and the rhythmic accompaniments suggest the endless motion of the mill wheel. Sing the song with attention to the rhythmic flow. Do not sing too loudly, but articulate clearly.

JOSEPHINE McGILL
Duna

"Duna" is a charming and nostalgic song by a little known composer. Its mood is that of remembrance and longing for earlier joys. The poem and music require no extensive analysis. Sing in a moving tempo, and color the voice appropriately to fit the poem.

SPIRITUAL, arr. GEORGE SHIRLEY
There is a Balm in Gilead

Many remarkable religious folk songs have come down to us from the early American Negroes. The Negro Spiritual is said to have originated in the religious camp meetings of the early slaves. No one knows who wrote the words or the music. Like other folk songs, they have been refined as they passed from one singer to another. "There is a Balm in Gilead" is one of the truly great and expressive spirituals. Sing it fervently, with a gentle rhythmic flow.

Observe the repeat and *D.S.* signs carefully. When you make the *Dal Segno* after the first verse, take the second ending of the refrain.

Aria: Ombra mai fù
(Serse)

Ombra mai fù
Di vegetabile
Cara ed amabile
Soave piu.

Never was there a shadow
Of branches
Sweeter, more refreshing
Or more gentle.

G.F. Handel

BAND 1

Om - - - bra mai_ fù di ve - ge -

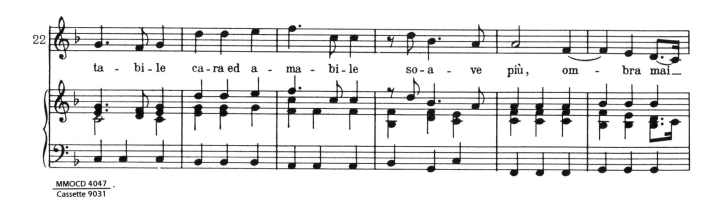

ta - bi - le ca - ra ed a - ma - bi - le so - a - ve più, om - bra mai_

MMOCD 4047
Cassette 9031

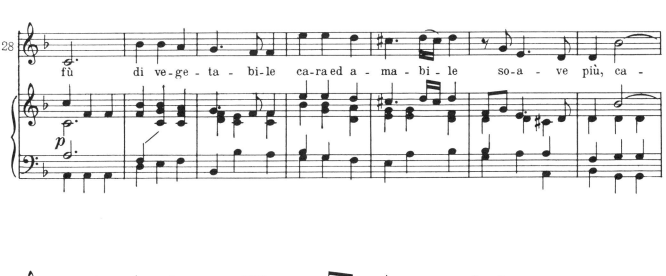

fù   di ve - ge - ta - bi - le   ca - ra ed a - ma - bi - le   so - a - ve più, ca -

- ra ed a - ma - bi - le, om - bra mai   fù   di ve - ge - ta - bi - le

ca - ra ed a - ma - bi - le so - a - ve più,   so - a - ve più.

MMOCD 4047
Cassette 9031

Cara, Cara e Dolce

Dear, dear and sweet liberty,
My soul, console yourself.
No longer live in servitude
If my heart, now free, departs

Fly hastily, yet remain near me.
Return, God of love;
My heart is already free
If my foot is no longer ensnared.

Alessandro Scarlatti

BAND 2

MMOCD 4047
Cassette 9031

6

tù S'il mio cor sciol-to s'en va
cor Se più lac ci il piè non hà

S'il mio cor sciol-to s'en va. Ca-ra, ca-ra e dol-ce
Se più lac-ci il pie non hà. Ca-ra, ca-ra e dol-ce

Ca-ra, ca-ra e dol-ce, ca-ra e dol-ce li-ber-tà. _____ Ca-ra e
Ca-ra, ca-ra e dol-ce, ca-ra e dol-ce li-ber-tà. _____ Ca-ra e

dol-ce li-ber-tà _____ Ca-ra e dol-ce li-ber-tà.
dol-ce li-ber-tà _____ Ca-ra e dol-ce li-ber-tà.

(a)

✱ In this performance, following a common practice, the introduction to the 2nd verse
begins on the 3rd beat of this measure.

If Music Be The Food of Love

BAND 3

High - G minor

Henry Purcell

nev - er cloy. Your eyes,_ your mien, your tongue de - clare That you__ are mu -
on - ly sound. Sure I__ must per - ish by__ your charms, Un - less__ you save__

(echo)
pp

- sic ev' - ry - where. Your eyes_ your mien,_ your tongue_ de - clare That
__ me in your arms. Sure I_ must per - ish by__ your charms, Un-

pp (echo)

una corda

dim.

1

2

you__ are mu - - sic ev' - ry where.
less_ you save ____ me in your v⸺ 2 Pleas - ures in - vade both arms.

dim.

tre corde

The Lovely Milleress
(Die Schöne Müllerin)
1 Wandering (Das Wandern)

BAND 4

Franz Schubert

wan - der, and _ wan - der, and _ wan - der, and _ wan - der.
wa - ter, the _ wa - ter, the _ wa - ter, the _ wa - ter.
Wan - dern, das _ Wan - dern, das _ Wan - dern, das _ Wan - dern.
Was - ser, das _ Was - ser, das _ Was - ser, das _ Was - ser.

3. The
4. The
5. O
3. Das
4. Die
5. O

cir - cling wheels have shown us _ how, The mill - wheels! The
mill - stones, heav - y though they _ be, The mill - stones! The
wan - d'ring, wan - d'ring, my _ de - light, O wan - d'ring! O
seh'n wir auch den Rä - dern _ ab, den Rä - dern, das
Stei - ne selbst, so schwer sie _ sind, die Stei - ne, die
Wan - dern, Wan - dern, mei - ne _ Lust, o Wan - dern! O

cir - cling wheels have shown us _ how, The mill - wheels! They
mill - stones, heav - y though they _ be, The mill - stones! They
wan - d'ring, wan - d'ring, my _ de - light, O wan - d'ring! Dear
seh'n wir auch den Rä - dern _ ab, den Rä - dern, die _
Stei - ne selbst, so schwer sie _ sind, die Stei - ne, sie
Wan - dern, Wan - dern, mei - ne _ Lust, o Wan - dern! Herr

Duna

Josephine McGill

I was a lit-tle lad With fol-ly on my lips, ___
(lass)

Fain was I for jour-ney-ing. All the seas in ships. But

now a - cross the south - ern swell, Ev - 'ry dawn I hear___ The

lit - tle streams of Du - na run - ning clear,___

The lit - tle streams of Du - na run - ning

clear.

sostenuto.

When I was a young man, Be - fore my beard was
(maid, And life was glad and

gray,— All to ships and sai - lor-men I gave my heart a -
gay,—)

-way, But I'm wea - ry of the sea - wind, I'm wea - ry of the

foam, And the lit - tle stars of Du - na, Call me home.—

The lit - tle stars of

Du - na call me home,_____ The lit - tle stars of

pp a tempo.

Du - na, Call me home._____

There Is a Balm in Gilead

MMO Compact Disc Catalog

BROADWAY

LES MISERABLES/PHANTOM OF THE OPERA	MMO CD 1016
HITS OF ANDREW LLOYD WEBBER	MMO CD 1054
GUYS AND DOLLS	MMO CD 1067
WEST SIDE STORY 2 CD Set	MMO CD 1100
CABARET 2 CD Set	MMO CD 1110
BROADWAY HEROES AND HEROINES	MMO CD 1121
CAMELOT	MMO CD 1173
BEST OF ANDREW LLOYD WEBBER	MMO CD 1130
THE SOUND OF BROADWAY	MMO CD 1133
BROADWAY MELODIES	MMO CD 1134
BARBRA'S BROADWAY	MMO CD 1144
JEKYLL & HYDE	MMO CD 1151
SHOWBOAT	MMO CD 1160
MY FAIR LADY 2 CD Set	MMO CD 1174
OKLAHOMA	MMO CD 1175
THE SOUND OF MUSIC 2 CD Set	MMO CD 1176
SOUTH PACIFIC	MMO CD 1177
THE KING AND I	MMO CD 1178
FIDDLER ON THE ROOF 2 CD Set	MMO CD 1179
CAROUSEL	MMO CD 1180
PORGY AND BESS	MMO CD 1181
THE MUSIC MAN	MMO CD 1183
ANNIE GET YOUR GUN 2 CD Set	MMO CD 1186
HELLO DOLLY! 2 CD Set	MMO CD 1187
OLIVER 2 CD Set	MMO CD 1189
SUNSET BOULEVARD	MMO CD 1193
GREASE	MMO CD 1196
SMOKEY JOE'S CAFE	MMO CD 1197
MISS SAIGON	MMO CD 1226

CLARINET

MOZART CONCERTO, IN A, K.622	MMO CD 3201
WEBER CONCERTO NO. 1 in Fm. STAMITZ CONC. No. 3 IN Bb	MMO CD 3202
SPOHR CONCERTO NO. 1 in C MINOR OP. 26	MMO CD 3203
WEBER CONCERTO OP. 26, BEETHOVEN TRIO OP. 11	MMO CD 3204
FIRST CHAIR CLARINET SOLOS	MMO CD 3205
THE ART OF THE SOLO CLARINET:	MMO CD 3206
MOZART QUINTET IN A, K.581	MMO CD 3207
BRAHMS SONATAS OP. 120 NO. 1 & 2	MMO CD 3208
WEBER GRAND DUO CONCERTANT WAGNER ADAGIO	MMO CD 3209
SCHUMANN FANTASY OP. 73, 3 ROMANCES OP. 94	MMO CD 3210
EASY CLARINET SOLOS Volume 1 - STUDENT LEVEL	MMO CD 3211
EASY CLARINET SOLOS Volume 2 - STUDENT LEVEL	MMO CD 3212
EASY JAZZ DUETS - STUDENT LEVEL	MMO CD 3213
BEGINNING CONTEST SOLOS - Jerome Bunke, Clinician	MMO CD 3221
BEGINNING CONTEST SOLOS - Harold Wright	MMO CD 3222
INTERMEDIATE CONTEST SOLOS - Stanley Drucker	MMO CD 3223
INTERMEDIATE CONTEST SOLOS - Jerome Bunke, Clinician	MMO CD 3224
ADVANCED CONTEST SOLOS - Stanley Drucker	MMO CD 3225
ADVANCED CONTEST SOLOS - Harold Wright	MMO CD 3226
INTERMEDIATE CONTEST SOLOS - Stanley Drucker	MMO CD 3227
ADVANCED CONTEST SOLOS - Stanley Drucker	MMO CD 3228
ADVANCED CONTEST SOLOS - Harold Wright	MMO CD 3229
BRAHMS Clarinet Quintet in Bm, Op. 115	MMO CD 3230
TEACHER'S PARTNER Basic Clarinet Studies	MMO CD 3231
JEWELS FOR WOODWIND QUINTET	MMO CD 3232
WOODWIND QUINTETS minus CLARINET	MMO CD 3233
FROM DIXIE to SWING	MMO CD 3234
THE VIRTUOSO CLARINETIST Baermann Method, Op. 63 4 CD Set	MMO CD 3240
ART OF THE CLARINET........... Baermann Method, Op. 64 4 CD Set	MMO CD 3241
POPULAR CONCERT FAVORITES WITH ORCHESTRA	MMO CD 3242
BAND-AIDS CONCERT BAND FAVORITES WITH ORCHESTRA	MMO CD 3243
TWENTY DIXIE CLASSICS	MMO CD 3824
TWENTY RHYTHM BACKGROUNDS TO STANDARDS	MMO CD 3825

PIANO

BEETHOVEN CONCERTO NO. 1 IN C	MMO CD 3001
BEETHOVEN CONCERTO NO. 2 IN Bb	MMO CD 3002
BEETHOVEN CONCERTO NO. 3 IN C MINOR	MMO CD 3003
BEETHOVEN CONCERTO NO. 4 IN G	MMO CD 3004
BEETHOVEN CONCERTO NO. 5 IN Eb (2 CD SET)	MMO CD 3005
GRIEG CONCERTO IN A MINOR OP.16	MMO CD 3006
RACHMANINOFF CONCERTO NO. 2 IN C MINOR	MMO CD 3007
SCHUMANN CONCERTO IN A MINOR	MMO CD 3008
BRAHMS CONCERTO NO. 1 IN D MINOR (2 CD SET)	MMO CD 3009
CHOPIN CONCERTO NO. 1 IN E MINOR OP. 11	MMO CD 3010
MENDELSSOHN CONCERTO NO. 1 IN G MINOR	MMO CD 3011
MOZART CONCERTO NO. 9 IN Eb K.271	MMO CD 3012
MOZART CONCERTO NO. 12 IN A K.414	MMO CD 3013
MOZART CONCERTO NO. 20 IN D MINOR K.466	MMO CD 3014
MOZART CONCERTO NO. 23 IN A K.488	MMO CD 3015
MOZART CONCERTO NO. 24 IN C MINOR K.491	MMO CD 3016

MOZART CONCERTO NO. 26 IN D K.537, CORONATION	MMO CD 3017
MOZART CONCERTO NO. 17 IN G K.453	MMO CD 3018
LISZT CONCERTO NO. 1 IN Eb, WEBER OP. 79	MMO CD 3019
LISZT CONCERTO NO. 2 IN A, HUNGARIAN FANTASIA	MMO CD 3020
J.S. BACH CONCERTO IN F MINOR, J.C. BACH CON. IN Eb	MMO CD 3021
J.S. BACH CONCERTO IN D MINOR	MMO CD 3022
HAYDN CONCERTO IN D	MMO CD 3023
HEART OF THE PIANO CONCERTO	MMO CD 3024
THEMES FROM GREAT PIANO CONCERTI	MMO CD 3025
TSCHAIKOVSKY CONCERTO NO. 1 IN Bb MINOR	MMO CD 3026
ART OF POPULAR PIANO PLAYING, Vol. 1 STUDENT LEVEL	MMO CD 3033
ART OF POPULAR PIANO PLAYING, Vol. 2 STUDENT LEVEL 2 CD Set	MMO CD 3034
'POP' PIANO FOR STARTERS STUDENT LEVEL	MMO CD 3035
DVORAK TRIO IN A MAJOR, OP. 90 "Dumky Trio"	MMO CD 3037
DVORAK QUINTET IN A MAJOR, OP. 81	MMO CD 3038
MENDELSSOHN TRIO IN D MAJOR, OP. 49	MMO CD 3039
MENDELSSOHN TRIO IN C MINOR, OP. 66	MMO CD 3040
BLUES FUSION FOR PIANO	MMO CD 3049
CLAUDE BOLLING SONATA FOR FLUTE AND JAZZ PIANO TRIO	MMO CD 3050
TWENTY DIXIELAND CLASSICS	MMO CD 3051
TWENTY RHYTHM BACKGROUNDS TO STANDARDS	MMO CD 3052
FROM DIXIE to SWING	MMO CD 3053
J.S. BACH BRANDENBURG CONCERTO NO. 5 IN D MAJOR	MMO CD 3054
BACH Cm CONC. for 2 PIANOS / SCHUMANN AND. & VAR., OP. 46 for 2 PIANOS	MMO CD 3055
J.C. BACH Bm CONC. / HAYDN C CONCERTINO / HANDEL CONC. GROSSO in D	MMO CD 3056
J.S. BACH TRIPLE CONCERTO IN A MINOR	MMO CD 3057
FRANCK SYM. VAR. / MENDELSSOHN: CAPRICCO BRILLANT	MMO CD 3058
C.P.E. BACH CONCERTO IN A MINOR	MMO CD 3059

PIANO - FOUR HANDS

RACHMANINOFF Six Scenes	4-5th year	MMO CD 3027
ARENSKY 6 Pieces, STRAVINSKY 3 Easy Dances	2-3rd year	MMO CD 3028
FAURE: The Dolly Suite		MMO CD 3029
DEBUSSY: Four Pieces		MMO CD 3030
SCHUMANN Pictures from the East	4-5th year	MMO CD 3031
BEETHOVEN Three Marches	4-5th year	MMO CD 3032
MOZART COMPLETE MUSIC FOR PIANO FOUR HANDS 2 CD Set		MMO CD 3036
MAYKAPAR First Steps, OP. 29	1-2nd year	MMO CD 3041
TSCHAIKOVSKY: 50 Russian Folk Songs		MMO CD 3042
BIZET: 12 Children's Games		MMO CD 3043
GRETCHANINOFF: ON THE GREEN MEADOW		MMO CD 3044
POZZOLI: SMILES OF CHILDHOOD		MMO CD 3045
DIABELLI: PLEASURES OF YOUTH		MMO CD 3046
SCHUBERT: FANTASIA & GRAND SONATA		MMO CD 3047

VIOLIN

BRUCH CONCERTO NO. 1 IN G MINOR OP.26	MMO CD 3100
MENDELSSOHN CONCERTO IN E MINOR	MMO CD 3101
TSCHAIKOVSKY CONCERTO IN D OP. 35	MMO CD 3102
BACH DOUBLE CONCERTO IN D MINOR	MMO CD 3103
BACH CONCERTO IN A MINOR, CONCERTO IN E	MMO CD 3104
BACH BRANDENBURG CONCERTI NOS. 4 & 5	MMO CD 3105
BACH BRANDENBURG CONCERTO NO. 2, TRIPLE CONCERTO	MMO CD 3106
BACH CONCERTO IN DM, (FROM CONCERTO FOR HARPSICHORD)	MMO CD 3107
BRAHMS CONCERTO IN D OP. 77	MMO CD 3108
CHAUSSON POEME, SCHUBERT RONDO	MMO CD 3109
LALO SYMPHONIE ESPAGNOLE	MMO CD 3110
MOZART CONCERTO IN D K.218, VIVALDI CON. AM OP. 3 NO. 6	MMO CD 3111
MOZART CONCERTO IN A K.219	MMO CD 3112
WIENIAWSKI CON. IN D. SARASATE ZIGEUNERWEISEN	MMO CD 3113
VIOTTI CONCERTO NO. 22 IN A MINOR	MMO CD 3114
BEETHOVEN 2 ROMANCES, SONATA NO. 5 IN F "SPRING SONATA"	MMO CD 3115
SAINT-SAENS INTRODUCTION & RONDO,	MMO CD 3116
MOZART SERENADE K. 204, ADAGIO K.261	
BEETHOVEN CONCERTO IN D OP. 61(2 CD SET)	MMO CD 3117
THE CONCERTMASTER - Orchestral Excerpts	MMO CD 3118
AIR ON A G STRING Favorite Encores with Orchestra Easy Medium	MMO CD 3119
CONCERT PIECES FOR THE SERIOUS VIOLINIST Easy Medium	MMO CD 3120
18TH CENTURY VIOLIN PIECES	MMO CD 3121
ORCHESTRAL FAVORITES - Volume 1 - Easy Level	MMO CD 3122
ORCHESTRAL FAVORITES - Volume 2 - Medium Level	MMO CD 3123
ORCHESTRAL FAVORITES - Volume 3 - Med to Difficult Level	MMO CD 3124
THE THREE B'S BACH/BEETHOVEN/BRAHMS	MMO CD 3125
VIVALDI Concerto in A Minor Op. 3 No. 6. in D Op. 3 No. 9.	
Double Concerto Op. 3 No. 8	MMO CD 3126
VIVALDI-THE FOUR SEASONS (2 CD Set)	MMO CD 3127
VIVALDI Concerto in Eb, Op. 8, No. 5. ALBINONI Concerto in A	MMO CD 3128
VIVALDI Concerto in E, Op. 3, No. 12. Concerto in C Op. 8, No. 6 "Il Piacere"	MMO CD 3129
SCHUBERT Three Sonatinas	MMO CD 3130
HAYDN String Quartet Op. 76 No. 1	MMO CD 3131
HAYDN String Quartet Op. 76 No. 2	MMO CD 3132
HAYDN String Quartet Op. 76 No. 3 "Emperor"	MMO CD 3133
HAYDN String Quartet Op. 76 No. 4 "Sunrise"	MMO CD 3134
HAYDN String Quartet Op. 76 No. 5	MMO CD 3135

MMO Music Group, 50 Executive Boulevard, Elmsford, New York 10523, 1 (800) 669-7464

6/6/97 PSG

MMO Compact Disc Catalog

HAYDN String Quartet Op. 76 No. 6 .... MMO CD 3136
BEAUTIFUL MUSIC FOR TWO VIOLINS 1st position, vol. 1 .... MMO CD 3137 ★
BEAUTIFUL MUSIC FOR TWO VIOLINS 2nd position, vol. 2 .... MMO CD 3138 ★
BEAUTIFUL MUSIC FOR TWO VIOLINS 3rd position, vol. 3 .... MMO CD 3139 ★
BEAUTIFUL MUSIC FOR TWO VIOLINS 1st, 2nd, 3rd position, vol. 4 .... MMO CD 3140 ★
TEACHER'S PARTNER Basic Violin Studies 1st year .... MMO CD 3142
DVORAK STRING TRIO "Terzetto", OP. 74 2 violins/viola .... MMO CD 3143
SIBELIUS VIOLIN Concerto in D Minor, OPUS 47 .... MMO CD 3144

★Lovely folk tunes and selections from the classics, chosen for their melodic beauty and technical value. They have been skillfully transcribed and edited by Samuel Applebaum, one of America's foremost teachers.

GUITAR

BOCCHERINI Quintet No. 4 in D "Fandango" .... MMO CD 3601
GIULIANI Quintet in A Op. 65 .... MMO CD 3602
CLASSICAL GUITAR DUETS .... MMO CD 3603
RENAISSANCE & BAROQUE GUITAR DUETS .... MMO CD 3604
CLASSICAL & ROMANTIC GUITAR DUETS .... MMO CD 3605
GUITAR AND FLUTE DUETS Volume 1 .... MMO CD 3606
GUITAR AND FLUTE DUETS Volume 2 .... MMO CD 3607
BLUEGRASS GUITAR .... MMO CD 3608
GEORGE BARNES GUITAR METHOD Lessons from a Master .... MMO CD 3609
HOW TO PLAY FOLK GUITAR 2 CD Set .... MMO CD 3610
FAVORITE FOLKS SONGS FOR GUITAR .... MMO CD 3611
FOR GUITARS ONLY! Jimmy Raney Small Band Arrangements .... MMO CD 3612
TEN DUETS FOR TWO GUITARS Geo. Barnes/Carl Kress .... MMO CD 3613
PLAY THE BLUES GUITAR A Dick Weissman Method .... MMO CD 3614
ORCHESTRAL GEMS FOR CLASSICAL GUITAR .... MMO CD 3615

FLUTE

MOZART Concerto No. 2 in D, QUANTZ Concerto in G .... MMO CD 3300
MOZART Concerto in G K.313 .... MMO CD 3301
BACH Suite No. 2 in B Minor .... MMO CD 3302
BOCCHERINI Concerto in D, VIVALDI Concerto in G Minor "La Notte", MOZART Andante for Strings .... MMO CD 3303
HAYDN Divertimento, VIVALDI Concerto in D Op. 10 No. 3 "Bullfinch", FREDERICK THE GREAT Concerto in C .... MMO CD 3304
VIVALDI Conc. in F; TELEMANN Conc. in D; LECLAIR Conc. in C .... MMO CD 3305
BACH Brandenburg No. 2 in F, HAYDN Concerto in D .... MMO CD 3306
BACH Triple Concerto, VIVALDI Concerto in D Minor .... MMO CD 3307
MOZART Quartet in F, STAMITZ Quartet in F .... MMO CD 3308
HAYDN 4 London Trios for 2 Flutes & Cello .... MMO CD 3309
BACH Brandenburg Concerti Nos. 4 & 5 .... MMO CD 3310
MOZART 3 Flute Quartets in D, A and C .... MMO CD 3311
TELEMANN Suite in A Minor, GLUCK Scene from 'Orpheus', PERGOLESI Concerto in G (2 CD Set) .... MMO CD 3312
FLUTE SONG: Easy Familiar Classics .... MMO CD 3313
VIVALDI Concerti In D, G, and F .... MMO CD 3314
VIVALDI Concerti in A Minor, G, and D .... MMO CD 3315
EASY FLUTE SOLOS Beginning Students Volume 1 .... MMO CD 3316
EASY FLUTE SOLOS Beginning Students Volume 2 .... MMO CD 3317
EASY JAZZ DUETS Student Level .... MMO CD 3318
FLUTE & GUITAR DUETS Volume 1 .... MMO CD 3319
FLUTE & GUITAR DUETS Volume 2 .... MMO CD 3320
BEGINNING CONTEST SOLOS Murray Panitz .... MMO CD 3321
BEGINNING CONTEST SOLOS Donald Peck .... MMO CD 3322
INTERMEDIATE CONTEST SOLOS Julius Baker .... MMO CD 3323
INTERMEDIATE CONTEST SOLOS Donald Peck .... MMO CD 3324
ADVANCED CONTEST SOLOS Murray Panitz .... MMO CD 3325
ADVANCED CONTEST SOLOS Julius Baker .... MMO CD 3326
INTERMEDIATE CONTEST SOLOS Donald Peck .... MMO CD 3327
ADVANCED CONTEST SOLOS Murray Panitz .... MMO CD 3328
ADVANCED CONTEST SOLOS Julius Baker .... MMO CD 3329
BEGINNING CONTEST SOLOS Doriot Anthony Dwyer .... MMO CD 3330
INTERMEDIATE CONTEST SOLOS Doriot Anthony Dwyer .... MMO CD 3331
ADVANCED CONTEST SOLOS Doriot Anthony Dwyer .... MMO CD 3332
FIRST CHAIR SOLOS with Orchestral Accompaniment .... MMO CD 3333
TEACHER'S PARTNER Basic Flute Studies 1st year .... MMO CD 3334
THE JOY OF WOODWIND MUSIC .... MMO CD 3335
JEWELS FOR WOODWIND QUINTET .... MMO CD 3336
BOLLING: SUITE FOR FLUTE/JAZZ PIANO TRIO .... MMO CD 3342
HANDEL / TELEMANN SIX SONATAS 2 CD Set .... MMO CD 3343
BACH SONATA NO. 1 in Bm / KUHLAU TWO DUETS in Em/D MAJOR 2 CD Set .... MMO CD 3344
KUHLAU TRIO for 3 FLUTES IN Eb, OP. 86 / BACH 2 SONATAS IN Eb/A 2 CD Set .... MMO CD 3345
PEPUSCH SONATA IN C / TELEMANN SONATA IN Cm .... MMO CD 3346
QUANTZ TRIO SONATA IN Cm / BACH GIGUE / ABEL SON. 2 IN F .... MMO CD 3347
TELEMANN CONCERTO NO. 1 IN D / CORRETTE SONATA IN E MINOR .... MMO CD 3348
TELEMANN TRIO IN F / Bb MAJOR / HANDEL SON. #3 IN C MAJOR .... MMO CD 3349
MARCELLO / TELEMANN / HANDEL SONATAS IN F MAJOR .... MMO CD 3350
CONCERT BAND FAVORITES WITH ORCHESTRA .... MMO CD 3351
BAND-AIDS CONCERT BAND FAVORITES WITH ORCHESTRA .... MMO CD 3352

RECORDER

PLAYING THE RECORDER Folk Songs of Many Naitons .... MMO CD 3337
LET'S PLAY THE RECORDER Beginning Children's Method .... MMO CD 3338
YOU CAN PLAY THE RECORDER Beginning Adult Method .... MMO CD 3339
3 SONATAS FOR FLUTE, HARPSICHORD & VIOLA DA GAMBA .... MMO CD 3340
3 SONATAS FOR ALTO RECORDER .... MMO CD 3341

FRENCH HORN

MOZART Concerti No. 2 & No. 3 in Eb. K. 417 & 447 .... MMO CD 3501
BAROQUE BRASS AND BEYOND .... MMO CD 3502
MUSIC FOR BRASS ENSEMBLE .... MMO CD 3503
MOZART Sonatas for Two Horns .... MMO CD 3504
BEGINNING CONTEST SOLOS Mason Jones .... MMO CD 3511
BEGINNING CONTEST SOLOS Myron Bloom .... MMO CD 3512
INTERMEDIATE CONTEST SOLOS Dale Clevenger .... MMO CD 3513
INTERMEDIATE CONTEST SOLOS Mason Jones .... MMO CD 3514
ADVANCED CONTEST SOLOS Myron Bloom .... MMO CD 3515
ADVANCED CONTEST SOLOS Dale Clevenger .... MMO CD 3516
INTERMEDIATE CONTEST SOLOS Mason Jones .... MMO CD 3517
ADVANCED CONTEST SOLOS Myron Bloom .... MMO CD 3518
INTERMEDIATE CONTEST SOLOS Dale Clevenger .... MMO CD 3519
FRENCH HORN WOODWIND MUSIC .... MMO CD 3520
MASTERPIECES FOR WOODWIND QUINTET .... MMO CD 3521
FRENCH HORN UP FRONT BRASS QUINTETS .... MMO CD 3522
HORN OF PLENTY BRASS QUINTETS .... MMO CD 3523
BAND-AIDS CONCERT BAND FAVORITES WITH ORCHESTRA .... MMO CD 3524

TRUMPET

THREE CONCERTI: HAYDN, TELEMANN, FASCH .... MMO CD 3801
TRUMPET SOLOS Student Level Volume 1 .... MMO CD 3802
TRUMPET SOLOS Student Level Volume 2 .... MMO CD 3803
EASY JAZZ DUETS Student Level .... MMO CD 3804
MUSIC FOR BRASS ENSEMBLE Brass Quintets .... MMO CD 3805
FIRST CHAIR TRUMPET SOLOS with Orchestral Accompaniment .... MMO CD 3806
THE ART OF THE SOLO TRUMPET with Orchestral Accompaniment .... MMO CD 3807
BAROQUE BRASS AND BEYOND Brass Quintets .... MMO CD 3808
THE COMPLETE ARBAN DUETS all of the classic studies .... MMO CD 3809
SOUSA MARCHES PLUS BEETHOVEN, BERLIOZ, STRAUSS .... MMO CD 3810
BEGINNING CONTEST SOLOS Gerard Schwarz .... MMO CD 3811
BEGINNING CONTEST SOLOS Armando Ghitalla .... MMO CD 3812
INTERMEDIATE CONTEST SOLOS Robert Nagel, Soloist .... MMO CD 3813
INTERMEDIATE CONTEST SOLOS Gerard Schwarz .... MMO CD 3814
ADVANCED CONTEST SOLOS Robert Nagel, Soloist .... MMO CD 3815
CONTEST SOLOS Armando Ghitalla .... MMO CD 3816
INTERMEDIATE CONTEST SOLOS Gerard Schwarz .... MMO CD 3817
ADVANCED CONTEST SOLOS Robert Nagel, Soloist .... MMO CD 3818
ADVANCED CONTEST SOLOS Armando Ghilalla .... MMO CD 3819
BEGINNING CONTEST SOLOS Raymond Crisara .... MMO CD 3820
BEGINNING CONTEST SOLOS Raymond Crisara .... MMO CD 3821
INTERMEDIATE CONTEST SOLOS Raymond Crisara .... MMO CD 3822
TEACHER'S PARTNER Basic Trumpet Studies 1st year .... MMO CD 3823
TWENTY DIXIELAND CLASSICS .... MMO CD 3824
TWENTY RHYTHM BACKGROUNDS TO STANDARDS .... MMO CD 3825
FROM DIXIE TO SWING .... MMO CD 3826
TRUMPET PIECES BRASS QUINTETS .... MMO CD 3827
MODERN BRASS QUINTETS .... MMO CD 3828
WHEN JAZZ WAS YOUNG The Bob Wilber All Stars .... MMO CD 3829
CONCERT BAND FAVORITES WITH ORCHESTRA .... MMO CD 3831
BAND-AIDS CONCERT BAND FAVORITES WITH ORCHESTRA .... MMO CD 3832

TROMBONE

TROMBONE SOLOS Student Level Volume 1 .... MMO CD 3901
TROMBONE SOLOS Student Level Volume 2 .... MMO CD 3902
EASY JAZZ DUETS Student Level .... MMO CD 3903
BAROQUE BRASS & BEYOND Brass Quintets .... MMO CD 3904
MUSIC FOR BRASS ENSEMBLE Brass Quintets .... MMO CD 3905
BEGINNING CONTEST SOLOS Per Brevig .... MMO CD 3911
BEGINNING CONTEST SOLOS Jay Friedman .... MMO CD 3912
INTERMEDIATE CONTEST SOLOS Keith Brown, Professor, Indiana University .... MMO CD 3913
INTERMEDIATE CONTEST SOLOS Jay Friedman .... MMO CD 3914
ADVANCED CONTEST SOLOS Keith Brown, Professor, Indiana University .... MMO CD 3915
ADVANCED CONTEST SOLOS Per Brevig .... MMO CD 3916
ADVANCED CONTEST SOLOS Keith Brown, Professor, Indiana University .... MMO CD 3917
ADVANCED CONTEST SOLOS Jay Friedman .... MMO CD 3918
ADVANCED CONTEST SOLOS Per Brevig .... MMO CD 3919
TEACHER'S PARTNER Basic Trombone Studies 1st year .... MMO CD 3920
TWENTY DIXIELAND CLASSICS .... MMO CD 3924
TWENTY RHYTHM BACKGROUNDS TO STANDARDS .... MMO CD 3925
FROM DIXIE TO SWING .... MMO CD 3926
STICKS & BONES BRASS QUINTETS .... MMO CD 3927
FOR TROMBONES ONLY MORE BRASS QUINTETS .... MMO CD 3928
POPULAR CONCERT FAVORITES The Stuttgart Festival Band .... MMO CD 3929
BAND-AIDS CONCERT BAND FAVORITES WITH ORCHESTRA .... MMO CD 3930

MMO Music Group, 50 Executive Boulevard, Elmsford, New York 10523, 1 (800) 669-7464

6/6/97 PSG

MMO Compact Disc Catalog

TENOR SAXOPHONE

CELLO

OBOE

ALTO SAXOPHONE

SOPRANO SAXOPHONE

BARITONE SAXOPHONE

VOCAL

DOUBLE BASS

DRUMS

VIOLA

VIBES

BASSOON

BANJO

TUBA or BASS TROMBONE

INSTRUCTIONAL METHODS

MMO Music Group, 50 Executive Boulevard, Elmsford, New York 10523, 1 (800) 669-7464   6/6/97 PSG

LAUREATE SERIES

Aria: Ombra mai fù
(Serse)

G.F. Handel

Om - - - bra mai fú   di ve-ge - ta - bi-le

Cara, Cara e Dolce

Alessandro Scarlatti

Allegretto grazioso   *p legato*   *mf*

Ca-ra, ca-ræ dol-ce   Ca-ra, ca-ræ

If Music Be the Food of Love

Henry Purcell

Gently   *p*   *cresc.*

If mu - sic be the food of love Sing on, sing on, sing

The Lovely Milleress
(Die Schöne Müllerin)
1. Wandering (Das Wandern)

Franz Schubert

Das   Wan –dern ist des   Mül-lers Lust, das   Wan – dern!   Das

Duna

Josephine McGill

When I   was   a   lit - tle lad   With   fol - ly on my

There Is A Balm in Gilead

Arranged by
George Shirley

There   is a   balm   in   Gi - le-ad   to

MMO MUSIC GROUP, INC., 50 Executive Boulevard, Elmsford, NY 10523-1325